Species Appropriate and Healthy Nutrition for Axolotls

ALINA DARIA

Contents

The Digestive Tract of the Axolotl

Axolotls have a rather flat and rounded head. When the mouth is closed, it might appear quite small - but appearances are deceptive, because the mouth can be opened wide and is quite big.

The mouths of axolotls are underslung (inferior). The underslung mouth is typical for animals that mainly look for their prey at the bottom of the water and usually stay there. With an underslung mouth, the lower jaw is shorter than the upper jaw and the opening of the mouth thus points downwards.

When not feeding, the axolotl's mouth is closed. However, if the axolotl keeps its mouth permanently open, something is usually wrong. The axolotl may have ingested too large a chunk of food, its stomach may be overloaded, or it may be infested with parasites such as nematodes. If the mouth is permanently open, the cause should definitely be identified.

As axolotls are pure carnivores, their digestive tract is dependent on animal food. Only this type of food can be completely digested and utilised by the animal. Vegetable food should therefore be avoided. This offers the axolotl no added value and is simply excreted without being utilised.

Axolotls can vomit. Since domesticated axolotls do not regulate their food intake themselves but eat almost everything that is offered to them by humans, the stomach can become overloaded, causing vomiting. Feeding too quickly or too frequently can also cause vomiting.

In this case, the amount of food should be reduced and the intervals between two feedings can be extended.

If an axolotl vomits, this can also be due to spoiled food. In any case, it should be checked whether the food is still fresh or, if in doubt, it should be disposed of.

A bacterial disease or parasite infestation can also trigger vomiting. If the axolotl has not ingested any spoiled food and the amount of food was definitely not too large, it should be examined whether the axolotl is possibly ill.

In addition, axolotls can also fall ill with diarrhoea, their faeces can be covered with mucus or blood can be found in the faeces. Such cases are almost always due to diseases such as infections, parasites, fungal diseases and the like. But swallowing stones can also cause blood in the faeces and, of course, constipation.

How often axolotls defecate depends mainly on their age. Young ones need food much more often than adult axolotls, so the young also defecate more frequently.

It is normal for very young axolotls (until they are about ten centimetres (four inches) big) to defecate every day. However, these animals are also fed daily. This is no longer the case with adult axolotls. Since adult axolotls eat less frequently, it is normal for them to defecate only about once or twice a week.

Occasionally, axolotls may swallow too much air. This happens quite often, especially with young axolotls. They then float close to the water surface and usually paddle around helplessly. This happens because there is too much air in the digestive tract and is usually caused by the axolotl being too greedy when taking in food and accidentally taking in too much air. Usually, this condition normalises itself and the axolotl lets the excess air escape.

However, if it does not manage to do this, the axolotl may need to be examined by a specialist vet who has experience with amphibians. Normally this is quite harmless and will quickly disappear. However, if it happens frequently, it should be checked whether the animal is getting enough food and whether the food is easily accessible.

The digestive tract of an axolotl is that of a carnivore. Therefore, the intestine only absorbs and utilises nutrients from animal food. Vegetable food components are not or hardly utilised. They pass through the intestine but are largely excreted unused.

A permanent feeding of plant food can also cause the intestine of an axolotl to become diseased, as it is simply not designed to have to process food other than animal food.

Axolotls have a cloaca - this is the common outlet of both the intestine and urinary bladder and the genital organ. Male axolotls have a larger cloaca than females. The cloaca of a male appears swollen (even if it is not actually swollen) and can therefore be easily identified with the naked eye.

The cloaca is part of the animal's rectum; not only excrement is excreted here, but also the sperm of the males and the eggs of the females.

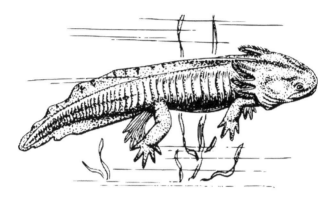

The physique of an axolotl.

© Open Clipart Vectors

Natural Foraging

Axolotls are nocturnal lurking hunters. Lurking hunters include carnivorous animals, which usually do not actively hunt and pursue their prey but remain in a certain place and wait there (patiently) for their prey. When the prey - for example, a small fish - swims past the axolotl, it attacks and grabs the prey animal.

To do this, the axolotl makes use of its electro and pressure receptors. For example, it has ampullary organs (ampullary receptors) and uses the lateral line system. This enables the axolotl to recognise or locate its prey.

When an animal moves in the water, this creates pressure fluctuations. The axolotl can perceive these with the help of its lateral line system.

Ampullary organs, on the other hand, perceive electro impulses that are generated by muscle activity. This also represents a stimulus for the axolotl and causes it to feed.

Axolotls are farsighted and therefore do not rely on their sense of sight when searching for food, but on the triggered stimuli described above to perceive food and to snatch it. Furthermore, the sense of smell is well developed and supports the animals in their search for food - especially when foraging on the ground.

Axolotls exercise a great deal of patience when lurking and sometimes remain in the same spot for hours in the wild. While a prey animal in an "active hunt" (chase) is aware that it is being pursued and accordingly tries to flee, the prey of the lurking hunters is usually surprised and does not expect an attack. Accordingly, lurking hunters have to expend much less energy than chasers, but of course they need a lot of patience and attention. Since axolotls need comparatively little food, this type of hunting is ideal for them.

They are "suction snappers". This means that they suck in their food suddenly and unexpectedly before the prey can flee. However, this is also practised when the prey is already dead or simply lying still.

However, axolotls do not only wait for prey to swim by, but also often collect their food from the bottom of the water. In the process, it can happen that the animals also suck in some substrate and this gets into their digestive tract.

For this reason, stones that are too large should not be used as substrate. In some countries, natural, rounded pebbles of a maximum size of three millimetres are used, in other countries, substrate is not used at all.

Fine sand is a good compromise, because it is better for the locomotion of the axolotl and for the bacterial balance in the aquarium if the bottom is covered. However, fine sand grains are of course very small, so that occasional swallowing does not pose a danger and does not cause blockages, as could be the case with larger stones.

The home of the axolotl near Mexico City.

© *Kin Enriquez*

The home of the axolotl near Mexico City.

© *Kin Enriquez*

Feeding Frequency

In the wild, axolotls often spend many hours looking for their food. As they are lurking hunters, they exercise a lot of patience and usually do not know when and how much prey can be hunted.

If domesticated axolotls live in a home aquarium, this is of course different. The rhythm of the feedings is determined by humans and the axolotls are not used to putting much effort into finding food. There are usually fixed feeding intervals and certain measured amounts of food. Nevertheless, axolotls retain their instincts, identify prey and snap at food, quite surprisingly. However, they are not used to life in the wild and know that food is put in front of them with a certain regularity. They therefore eat just about everything that humans offer them and do not regulate their food intake independently. It is therefore the human's responsibility to control the axolotl's food intake, to provide a varied diet and to keep an eye on the weight.

Exact recommendations for feeding intervals and quantities are quite difficult to give, as the needs depend very much on the size and age of the animal, and as the animals are of course individual. Since axolotls living together in a group should have approximately the same body size, their food requirements are often quite similar. It is even better if the animals are about the same age. It has been observed that axolotls get a slower metabolism with increasing age and that the speed of metabolism decreases from year to year.

Young animals need food more often than adult axolotls. They should be fed daily and usually defecate daily as well.

As a general rule of thumb ...

... with a body size of up to 12 centimetres (4.7 inches), axolotls can be fed every day;

... with a body size of up to about 16 centimetres (6.3 inches), they can be fed every two days;

... with a body size of up to about 18 centimetres (7 inches), they can be fed every three days;

... with a body size of more than 18 centimetres (more than 7 inches), they can be fed once or twice a week - many owners feed their adult animals only once a week.

It should be noted, however, that these are only guidelines. Axolotls should always be observed so that the appropriate amount of food and the time intervals slowly settle in. If an axolotl loses weight, the amount of food should be increased. If it gains weight, however, it must be reduced - or more fasting days must be taken. Excess weight in an axolotl should be taken very seriously, as this can lead to organ fatty degeneration (e.g., fatty degeneration of the liver) and consequently to further diseases.

Fasting periods of one to two weeks are usually considered problem-free (for adult axolotls). Therefore, the owners can go away for the weekend or take a short holiday without necessarily having someone come home to feed the animals. When the fasting phase is too long is quite controversial in the axolotl community.

However, the general principle is that two weeks without food should not be exceeded, as otherwise the animals could start attacking each other and maiming or injuring themselves. If you are going on a two- or three-week holiday, it is a good idea to have someone come home once or twice during this time to feed the animals. After all, this does not take up a lot of time.

A fully grown axolotl. © *Tinwe*

Fresh Food and Live Feed

Fresh food is the most species-appropriate diet for axolotls, as animals in the wild naturally also feed on fresh food.

As food, axolotls in the wild use just about anything that they can overpower and that fits in their mouths. This mainly includes insects, worms, insect larvae, small fish, fish fry, small snails and small crustaceans.

Feeding the axolotl should be varied and you should not limit yourself to just one or two different foods, as otherwise there is a risk of massive nutrient deficiencies!

In the following we will take a closer look at some well-known foods for axolotls:

1. European night crawler (Eisenia hortensis, Dendrobena veneta)

2. Dew worm (Lumbricus terrestris)

3. Mosquito larvae

4. Freshwater shrimp (Gammarus)

5. Artemia salina (Brine shrimp)

6. Maggots

7. Tubifex (River worm, Sewage worm)

8. Crickets

1. The European night crawler belongs to the earthworms, of which there are about three thousand different species worldwide. It is usually called *dendrobena* and is rightly considered one of the best and tastiest foods for axolotls. As the name suggests, the dendrobena is red. It is quite a large worm, which

should be cut up before feeding if necessary, for smaller axolotls. A worm that is to be fed must not extend more than from the axolotl's mouth to its cloaca. If in doubt, it is a good idea to cut the worm in half to make it easier to eat. Dendrobenas consist of about 85% water, 11% protein and 1.5% fat. Their nutrient content is therefore almost identical to that of dew worms, which makes them a healthy food for axolotls.

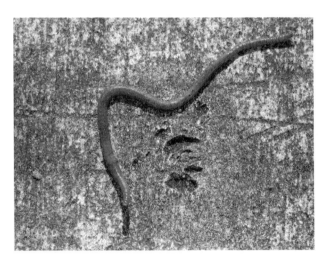

© *iGlobalWeb*

2. The dew worm is also very popular with axolotls. It is the "common earthworm" and is most common in Europe. It is also quite long and should be cut in half before feeding to make it easier for the axolotl to eat. The dew worm is lighter in colour than the dendrobena and has a light reddish or brownish colour. Dew worms have a pleasingly low fat content and are quite rich in nutrients, which makes them an ideal food for axolotls. They consist of about 80% water, about 12% protein and only about 1.5% fat.

© *Natfot*

3. Mosquito larvae are mainly used for rearing young axolotls. To feed an adult axolotl with mosquito larvae, quite a large quantity is necessary. Although they should not be the main food for adult axolotls, there is nothing wrong with adding mosquito larvae to the food for greater dietary diversity. You can choose between black, red and white mosquito larvae. Mosquito larvae contain a lot of water (black mosquito larva 81%, red mosquito larva 87% and white mosquito larva 90%) and very little fat.

4. Freshwater shrimps (Gammarus) are not usually offered as live food, as this would make both storage and transport more difficult. Freshwater shrimp are ideally bought dried, sometimes they are also offered as frozen food. Compared to the previously described foods, freshwater shrimp are higher in fat and should therefore not make up the main diet; however, they are very suitable as a regular food supplement. The crude protein content of Freshwater shrimp is about 30-50% and the fat content is about 5-6%. In addition, freshwater shrimp are very rich in fibre, consisting of

about 20-25% crude fibre. Fibre is particularly good for healthy digestion and "cleans" the intestinal walls!

5. Artemia salina are also small crustaceans, often also called brine shrimp. They belong to the "gill-foot" crustaceans. Artemias are quite small, and young crustaceans are usually used for feeding - also because they are particularly rich in nutrients. But even adult ones remain quite small with a size of about one and a half centimetres (approx. 0.5 inches). The nutrient content of Artemia is similar to the nutrient content of freshwater shrimp, as they also have about 25% crude fibre and about 5-6% fat. The crude protein content is usually around 40-45%. Therefore, these small crustaceans are also well suited for feeding axolotls.

6. Maggots can be found in every fishing shop and also often in pet shops. They are not only popular with many fish species, but also with axolotls. Compared to the foods presented so far, however, they are quite high in calories, so maggots should - if at all - only be offered as a snack now and then. Before feeding, the maggot

should ideally be scratched, as the carapace is quite hard, and the axolotl might otherwise not be able to digest the maggot. Maggots will be ok for about a month in the fridge or in a similarly cool place. The same applies to mealworms - these are even more calorific than maggots and contain hardly any nutrients. Although they do not harm the axolotl directly, they are little fatteners (fat content about 20-35%) and offer no real added value to the diet. Therefore, mealworms can be safely dispensed with.

Maggots and mealworms are little fatteners.

7. Tubifex are also called "river worms" or "sewage worms". They belong to the annelids and can even grow up to nine centimetres long (approx. 3.5 inches). However, they are very thin. Tubifex can generally be found in any large pet shop, as they are not only popular as axolotl food, but also as food for various fish species. They can be purchased live, dried or in frozen form. However, many axolotl keepers decide against Tubifex as a live food, as several cases have already been reported in which live Tubifex have transmitted pathogens to the animals. For this reason, Tubifex are quite controversial among aquarists.

8. Crickets (house crickets) have a high protein content and also consist of about 10% dietary fibre. However, it should also be noted that crickets are quite high in fat, as the fat content is about 13-15%. They can therefore be offered from time to time as a supplement and for variety; however, they are not necessary for a healthy feeding of the axolotl and are only considered a small snack.

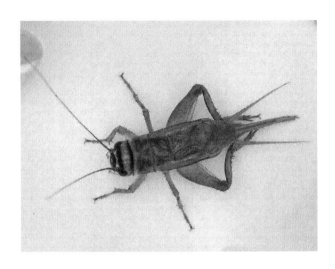

House cricket. © *Hans Braxmeier*

It is difficult to socialise axolotls with other species. In principle, axolotls should only live in pure aquariums, i.e., there should only be other axolotls in the aquarium. The only creatures that can (but do not have to!) live together with axolotls are ...

... endler's guppies (Poecilia wingei);

... dwarf shrimps (Neocaridina);

... bubble snails (Physidae);

... post horn snails (Planorbarius corneus);

... cardinal fish (Tanichthys albonubes);

... and zebra danios (Danio rerio).

However, it should be noted that the previously mentioned creatures are regarded as food by the axolotls and will be eaten by them sooner or later. This of course makes it more difficult to regulate the food intake and the creatures usually turn out to be relatively expensive live food.

Furthermore, it is also an ethical question whether one wants to keep the species mentioned in the axolotl aquarium at all - knowing that they will be eaten at an undetermined time. There are countries where the feeding of live food is not allowed anyway.

All other species are not allowed to live together with axolotls under any circumstances. This often leads to avoidable accidents, sometimes resulting in the death of one or both animals. It is important to understand that axolotls will eat almost anything that fits in their mouths - and they often make mistakes. If a fish is too big to eat, this often does not stop the axolotl from trying anyway. These are natural reflexes. It can happen that the fish gets stuck in the axolotl's mouth or throat and both animals die.

It is particularly dangerous to keep them together with catfish - a catfish is usually too big to be eaten and almost always gets stuck. However, it also has barbs on its head that make such an accident even more dangerous. The barbs get stuck in the mouth of the axolotl and injure both animals. It has often happened that both animals died in such an accident because the catfish could not be removed. In addition, there are fish species that like to nibble at the tail or gills of axolotls, sometimes causing them extreme damage. Goldfish, for example, are known for this behaviour.

It should also be mentioned that axolotl eggs and juveniles are also considered live food. Axolotls do not build up emotional relationships. They often eat their own laid eggs if these have not already been removed from the aquarium by humans. If the eggs hatch, the juveniles usually also end up as live food for the adult axolotls sooner or later.

As described above, axolotls identify their prey mainly by their sense of smell and by stimuli such as pressure waves in the water - and snap at the prey. They do not distinguish whether it is a small fish or possibly a young axolotl. You should be aware of this before acquiring axolotls.

If there are both female and male axolotls in the aquarium, the laid eggs can be removed by humans. However, these must be frozen before disposal so that they die. Whether one finds this morally acceptable is an individual decision.

If you do not want to remove the eggs or raise the young separately or release them for eating, it is advisable to keep only axolotls of the same gender. This avoids this problem, because many people do not want to breed or dispose of the eggs, nor do they want to leave the young in the aquarium with the large axolotls. From an ethical point of view, this is completely understandable.

Frozen Food

The best, most natural and species-appropriate food for axolotls is fresh food, as axolotls also feed on fresh food in the wild. However, purely fresh feeding is not possible for all people who would like to look after axolotls. Frozen food offers an acceptable alternative here. It can, of course, also be offered as a supplement to fresh food.

Frozen food should be as natural as possible. As a rule, the important nutrients in the food are well preserved, as it is naturally frozen and only thawed when necessary.

Frozen food is usually offered especially for fish. In principle this is not a problem, but you should make sure that the food composition is also suitable for axolotls.

Many types of frozen food contain artemia, freshwater shrimp, mosquito larvae and similar. This corresponds to a healthy diet for the axolotl.

Some frozen foods are offered ready portioned, others in "large blocks". Both variants are fine, because even larger blocks can be portioned well with the help of a sharp knife.

However, it is important that only as much food is defrosted as is necessary for feeding. No more food should be thawed than is needed - and even more so, it should not be refrozen once it has started to thaw. The rotting process of frozen food begins as soon as it starts to thaw. It is therefore important to feed the frozen food quickly and not wait too long.

Furthermore, it should be rinsed well before feeding, as sometimes there are excrements or similar in the food that should not get into the aquarium. A fine sieve is particularly suitable for this purpose!

As already explained, most axolotl keepers use either very fine gravel or sand as substrate. Some do not use any substrate at all.

If there is no substrate in the aquarium or if sand is used (recommended!), feeding frozen food is no problem. However, if gravel is used, this type of feeding can be difficult. The ingredients of most frozen foods are quite small, so they can easily get lost between and among the pebbles. There is also an increased risk that the axolotls will swallow the gravel.

Of course, frozen fish is also part of the frozen food. This can be bought in the frozen section of any supermarket. However, it is important that the frozen fish is not seasoned or otherwise processed!

Also, the frozen fish should not have any bones. If it does have bones, these must be removed before feeding. Fish should also be portioned before thawing and fed quickly after thawing.

Larger fish fillets must be cut into bite-sized pieces before feeding so that the axolotl does not choke on them and so that the fish does not get stuck. A size of about 1 cm x 3 cm is recommended (approx. 0.4 inches x 1.2 inches). Ideally, each axolotl should be given five to six of these bite-sized pieces per feeding. If worms, small crustaceans, pellets or small snails are also fed, the quantities should be adjusted individually.

The fish species should be freshwater fish. With sea / saltwater fish, there is a risk that the axolotl will be given (too much) iodine, as these fish contain a lot of iodine due to their origin. This should be avoided in any case, as iodine can trigger metamorphosis. Axolotls remain in the larval stage throughout their lives because they have a thyroid defect that prevents metamorphosis - i.e., transformation into an "adult" amphibian. Metamorphosis in axolotls can be induced by the external administration of artificial hormones - and this can also happen when feeding (too much) iodine.

Suitable fish species for feeding to axolotls include **trout, zander, perch and pike.**

Leftover food can and should be removed with the help of feeding tongs.

Fresh fish that must first be cut up.

© *Andreas Lischka*

Pellets, industrial dried food

Fresh food is the best choice for feeding axolotls, as this is what they naturally feed on in the wild. Frozen food can partly replace fresh food or at least complement it well. Pellets or industrially produced dry food are not usually necessary, as such food does not correspond to the natural diet of axolotls. However, there are cases in which pellets must be used or in which pellets can be offered as a supplement.

If you want to feed pellets, pay close attention to the composition of the ingredients. The qualitative differences between the individual products are sometimes huge. There are pellets on the market that contain only 20-30% fish. These are not at all suitable for an axolotl, as the axolotl is a carnivore. For example, there are pellets on the market with a raw protein content of over 50% - these are well suited as supplementary food.

Unhealthy additives should also not be found in the pellets. Many industrial animal feeds, for example, are enriched with "vegetable by-products" to keep costs down. This is a nicer word for "waste". Vegetable by-products are generated during the production of other products. To prevent them from going to waste, they are added to animal feed, for example. This is also often the case with rodent food. The same applies to "animal by-products".

Vegetable by-products offer no added value for axolotls. They are neither healthy nor species-appropriate, as axolotls are of course not herbivores or omnivores. These ingredients are excreted again anyway without being used.

Nevertheless, it must be mentioned that pellets entirely without any plant ingredients are not offered at this time. A small component of plant ingredients is necessary to hold the individual components of the pellets together, as they act like a "glue".

These ingredients are small individual particles that slowly dissolve in the water if the pellets are not eaten by the axolotls. If pellets are offered, they must be eaten quickly by the animals, otherwise there is a risk of extreme contamination of the aquarium water. If individual pellets are not eaten, they should be removed from the aquarium within an hour.

Pellets should never be the sole food of the axolotl, as this would simply be too one-sided and unhealthy. If pellets are used, they should make up a maximum of one fifth or one quarter of the total food quantity. Otherwise, there is a risk of nutrient deficiency in the animals. The animal components of the pellets should make up at least 45%.

Pellets. © Cecep Risnandar

Food from Nature – Yes or No?

There are some axolotl keepers who look for food for their animals in the wild. This primarily involves worms such as earthworms.

Whether this is recommendable is highly controversial. I personally do not recommend it. On the one hand, axolotls don't eat very much and not very often - so it actually makes little or no difference to your finances whether you collect food for the axolotls in the wild or not. The financial aspects are negligible, also because worms can be grown / bred quite easily at home. Many axolotl keepers breed their own earthworms in a box or bucket, for example. This minimises the risk of pathogens or harmful substances.

In addition, collected food from the wild offers no more value compared to purchased or home-bred fresh worms. The little animals from the wild are not better or more nutritious than the purchased feed, as long as they are alive / fresh.

Personally, I don't see any advantage in collecting worms and other food in nature. However, I do see some disadvantages and dangers.

Live food can introduce parasites and other pathogens into the axolotl's aquarium. With a carnivorous animal like the axolotl, the risk of this is always higher than with an herbivorous animal like guinea pigs, rabbits, etc. - because parasites often use worms and insects as intermediate hosts on which they nest for a while. If food containing pathogens is introduced into the axolotl aquarium, these pathogens and parasites will quite quickly pass on to the axolotl group and use them as hosts.

Of course, this is also possible if the food is bought or home-bred. As a rule, such a risk cannot be ruled out. However, the risk is higher if the food is collected in the wild.

Other toxins could also be accidentally introduced into the aquarium if the feed is obtained from the wild. Here, of course, it depends in which areas and on which land is collected. Pesticides, rat poisons and other harmful substances are a real risk that can be avoided.

An earthworm on the grass.

© *Sarah Harding*

Excess Weight

Adult axolotls need to be fed less frequently than many other popular pets - therefore it happens that some owners "mean too well with their animals" and overfeed them. Overfeeding is quite common and should be avoided at all costs.

In order to determine the optimal food dose and the optimal intervals, the animals must be well observed. An axolotl should always maintain its normal weight. Of course, it should not lose weight, but weight problems are usually due to the fact that axolotls get too much food instead of too little. The belly should be about as wide as the axolotl's head - then the axolotl usually has a normal weight.

An overweight axolotl is prone to organ fatty degeneration. This primarily affects the liver. Fatty organs and general overweight also provide ideal circumstances for other diseases.

Overweight is indeed a frequent cause of death in domesticated amphibians. Therefore, if weight gain occurs, more fasting days should be taken. If the axolotl still does not lose weight or if the overweight affects only one axolotl in the group, it is likely that the weight gain is due to other diseases. Research into the causes should be carried out by an experienced vet.

It is not only too frequent feeding that can cause overweight, but also too much food and, above all, food that is too rich in fat.

Sometimes other circumstances are mistaken for obesity. This happens, for example, when an axolotl has eaten (many) stones and these accumulate in the abdomen. In the worst case, these stones cannot be excreted and cause - sometimes fatal - blockages. Therefore, it is essential that the substrate consists of very small stones or, at best, fine sand, so that accidentally eaten substrate can be excreted again. Larger stones that fit into the mouth of the axolotl should be strictly avoided.

Abdominal dropsy (ascites) is sometimes mistaken for obesity. Dropsy is quite common in amphibians - and also in fish - and is strictly speaking not a disease in itself, but the symptom or consequence of an organ disease.

If an animal is affected by dropsy, a lot of water sometimes accumulates throughout the body - mainly in the abdominal cavity, of course. There are many reasons for this; for example, a bacterial infection can trigger dropsy.

The organs no longer work properly and, in some cases, if the disease is far advanced, have even given up (kidney failure / kidney hypofunction). It is imperative that dropsy is examined and treated by a veterinarian who knows amphibians. Usually antibiotics are necessary, sometimes drainage tablets are also used. Nevertheless, it is essential not only to treat the dropsy itself, but primarily to get to the bottom of the cause.

Legal Notice

This book is protected by copyright. Reproduction by third parties is prohibited. Use or distribution by unauthorised third parties in any printed, audio-visual, audio or other media is prohibited. All rights remain solely with the author.

Author: Alina Daria Djavidrad

Contact: Wiesenstr. 6, 45964 Gladbeck, Germany

© 2021 Alina Daria Djavidrad

1st edition (2021)

Room for Notes

Made in the USA
Middletown, DE
01 October 2021

49451358R00033